The Spiritual Family

John-Roger

Books by John-Roger

Spiritual Warrior—The Art of Spiritual Success
Inner Worlds of Meditation
The Tao of Spirit
Forgiveness: The Key to the Kingdom
The Christ Within & The Disciples of Christ
  with the Cosmic Christ Calendar
Dream Voyages
Walking with the Lord
God Is Your Partner
Q&A from the Heart
Passage Into Spirit
Relationships—The Art of Making Life Work
Loving—Each Day
Wealth & Higher Consciousness
The Power Within You
The Spiritual Promise
The Sound Current
The Signs of the Times
The Way Out Book
Sex, Spirit & You
Possessions, Projections & Entities
The Path to Mastership
Music is the Message
The Master Chohans of the Color Rays
Manual on Using the Light
The Journey of a Soul
Dynamics of the Lower Self
Drugs
The Consciousness of Soul
Buddha Consciousness
Blessings of Light
Baraka
Awakening Into Light

For further information, please contact:
Mandeville Press®
P.O. Box 513935
Los Angeles, CA 90051-1935
(213) 737-4055

Contents

1. Husbands & Wives *1*
2. And Kids *51*
3. Love and Discipline *91*
4. Family and Home *133*
   Bibliography 166

| M |

Mandeville Press
P.O. Box 513935
Los Angeles, CA 90051-1935

©1976, 1997
Peace Theological Seminary
& College of Philosophy

All rights reserved, including the right
of reproduction in whole
or in part in any form.

Printed in the United States of America

Library of Congress Catalog Card
Number: 76-17344

I.S.B.N. 0-914829-21-1

Chapter 1

Husbands

&

Wives

In the whole action of being together and living here on this planet earth, marriage has become a very important concept, and the concept of the family even more important. In the marriage pattern, the husband and wife come together to learn from one another, to grow together into their highest expression. Too often, however, one (or both) looks at the other one as a *possession*—"now he belongs to me" or "she's mine."

Historically women have been looked upon as chattels, as being owned by men—or even owned by the society. And men haven't done too much to stop that particular type of approach; rather, they have perpetrated it.

It's quite true that this day and age is "a man's world." That doesn't necessarily mean that it has to be a masculine world, however. Far, far back in history, it was the female consciousness that ruled the planet and had what we call the male consciousness in total subservience. The women did rather horrendous things for which they became karmically responsible. Karmic law won't be mocked—it must be fulfilled. So there was a period when the female consciousness became disenfranchised. They lost their rights. Man, in his far memory of that ancient action, but without conscious knowledge of it, kept pushing women further and further down into subservience, as if to say, "I'll get you so low that you'll never be able to rise up again and overthrow me and make me the slave again."

In the New Age we are entering, there is more and more of a balance coming forward. Some of it is because of the feminist movement; total credit or discredit can't really be placed there any more than it can be placed anywhere else, however. It's just that the consciousnesses of both men and women are changing, and there is more of an equality coming forward. The liberationists are saying, "There are some things that women should be able to have and to hold as rightfully as men." That is absolutely true, absolutely valid.

The Spirit of the Aquarian age, into which many people say we are moving, is not to label and categorize and in that way separate, but to move into a oneness of consciousness. It is not to look upon people as chairmen or chairwomen or chairpersons, but to look upon them as manifestations of that consciousness of leadership, and to give them the respect they earn according to their ability and their demonstration of responsibility.

That respect is earned by getting out and *doing*. That's all it is. When there is something that needs to be done, it doesn't matter who does it—man or woman. It needs to be done by one who has the ability and the responsibility to complete it.

Many men and women experience a rather deep-seated distrust of the members of the opposite sex. The origin of those feelings is valid; it comes through the ancient memories of many wrongs over many eons of time. The consciousness present in your body right now—whether it is male or female—has been present many times. It has been both male and female. When you realize that, you realize that neither one is truly superior or inferior to the other. They are different from one another. Neither is better or worse. Men and women exist on a horizontal line, not a vertical hierarchy.

Much of the process of liberation, as you attempt to stand up inside of yourself and say, "I am a free individual," is simply the demonstration of the responsibility of being free. Those people who sit in the midst of their despair, crying out about their suppression, should stand up and yell. At least they would be assuming a certain responsibility for their suppression. Instead of sitting there and "chewing their guts into fiddle strings," they might stand up and say, "I feel that I am being mistreated, and I would prefer not to be treated this way. If you can't go along with my preference, and I can't get out of the situation, then I will go along with you. I want to put you on notice that you're going to have a struggle, however. The struggle will be *me* attempting to get out of this and *you* attempting to hold me back." This is part of the age-old struggle.

When a man and a woman enter into the marriage pattern, the man-woman struggle that is the archetype of society starts manifesting within the marriage. One attempts to become the authority figure of the family. That one functions under the negative power, the magnetic power, and may set up rules and regulations for suppression—which is the manifestation of negativity. If the rules and regulations are guidelines for the freedom of the entire family, then they are stepping-stones, not stumbling-blocks. There does need to be guidelines in any family, whether it's just husband and wife or whether there are also children involved. But it should be understood by everyone that the guidelines are there to protect and assist, not to restrict. People who are working closely with one another (as a family, as business partners, as friends, etc.) have a certain responsibility to one another. That responsibility is basically that they work together for the highest good of the group, that they are willing to cooperate with one another to bring about the highest good, and that they keep love present—all the time.

I have four young friends who work very closely with one another. One day they were preparing some land for planting, and were throwing out a combination of mineral dusts. They got carried away with the fun of it all and ended up in a "fight" with each other, until everyone was completely covered with dust. Then they carried the rough-and-tumble over towards the swimming pool and tried to push one another into the pool to get cleaned off. In the midst of all this, one of them fell and hurt his hand rather badly. Fun is fun, but as soon as someone gets hurt, there are several things that take place. One is that the person who is hurt can't hold up his end of the work load, so that becomes a hardship on the others—and on himself. Another thing is that now everyone feel badly that the "horseplay" extended out so far that it hurt someone. The third thing is that when one gets hurt, the others are hurt, too. If a husband sprains his ankle and can't sleep at night because of the pain, the wife's going to have difficulty sleeping, too, because they share the same bed. Maybe she's the one who has to get up and get the ice pack and the aspirin and whatever else he needs. Because these things are shared, people in families have responsibilities to one another. If one spouse gets hurt, the other one, even if out of pure selfishness, should get busy and help the spouse get better as fast as possible. It'll be worth it. If others are not smart enough to take care of themselves, you do it for them because they're part of you.

You should never look for perfection in marriage. Marriage is not perfect, although hopefully, it's moving that way. In the meantime, it's sandpapering. It's getting the diamond out of the rough, polishing it, and putting it in a beautiful setting. But you don't have to use blacksmith's tools to do it. You don't have to chip or cut or hit. You just smoothly sandpaper. And you don't have to complete the entire job in one day. You can do it over a period of time. Sometimes the journey is more fun than getting there. I'm sure most fellows understand that sometimes the cruising around and looking is more fun than finding someone and having sex. It may take all night to find someone and a few minutes later, it's all over. Moving towards it is the adventurous consciousness of seeking, and that can be fun. But the interesting thing is that a rat has the same consciousness of seeking. So at some point, it is really nice to lift yourself above the animal consciousness and manifest a higher expression.

It is part of man's nature to look and see what's available. Men do this, and women will be further ahead if they accept that men do look. If the man you're married to or living with looks at another woman, keep in mind that he may not really be interested in her; he may only be comparing and be so thankful for what he has. So don't accuse him before the fact. There are only a few things that are sacred in marriage, and opinion is not one of them—neither is supposition. The facts and the truths are really sacred; not the interpretations—just what *is*.

Women may look around at attractive men, too. There's nothing that says she can't look—just like there's nothing that says he can't look. She may just be looking at reference points and thinking, "Thank God I've got you." But if she turns around to give you a hug filled with love and you're ready to slug her in the face for looking, you've lost. If you hit her, and she says, "Thanks, I needed that," take her to the psychiatric ward. If you hit her for looking, she should probably turn around and land one on your eye so you can keep up the "twin" consciousness. What's good for the goose is good for the gander—and don't forget it.

If men think they can go to bed with women as some sort of "spiritual action," don't think she can't do the same "spiritual action" with somebody else. This idea of passing off a sexual encounter as a "spiritual action" is the biggest bunch of nonsense that you'll ever hear coming out of somebody. If a couple says, "I like it and you like it so let's do it," at least that's honest. One of them may add, "I'm only going to do it with you once because I've got a whole list here. You're forty-two and the list is five thousand. So let's get on with it." The other one may say, "Fine, you're twenty-nine on my list of ten thousand."

Without love there's nothing very special about sex. With love it can be very, very special. But that one you love, you love for many reasons and on many levels—and that's what makes it special. Sex alone is just an exchange between two bodies, and bodies are pretty much alike. Some may be fatter or thinner or going bald or too hairy or whatever, but basically they're pretty much the same. So keep in mind that it's the love that counts, not just the sex.

If you hold to the truths, the facts, your marriage will be in pretty good shape. It is so easy to assert an ego consciousness against your spouse and come on as the authority. Be very careful in your marriage that you don't draw conclusions towards an end that doesn't exist. Go on the facts. Go on what is, and you'll be okay. Keep in mind that things are not always what they appear to be. If your husband comes home from work, barely mumbles "hello" and then turns on the TV, don't jump to the conclusion that he's upset with you or doesn't love you. Check it out. Ask him if he's upset. Ask him if he's had a bad day at the office. Rub his shoulders. Let him know you care. Love him. But if he wants to be left alone, leave him alone. That can be love, too. This idea also works in reverse. If the husband comes home and his wife is pretty quiet, check to see if anything's wrong that you need to talk about. Let her know you love her and that you care. When you take care of each other in a total, loving consciousness, then neither one can ever go anywhere that will be better than home.

There is a responsibility in marriage to stay healthy and do those things that will enhance your health. When children appear in the marriage, you must make sure that they eat properly and get the proper rest and exercise so they are healthy, too. If the children get sick and the wife stays up night after night after night taking care of them, then she may end up in the hospital. The husband then has to hire someone to take care of the children while he works overtime to pay the doctor bills. And the kids are upset because their Mom is sick and their Dad is gone all the time. How good has martyrdom been? If the children are sick, let the husband get up some of the nights; let him sit up with them. He is part of the creation; he also has responsibility of maintenance and repair. If you are going to bring children into this world, you enter into the responsibility of their maintenance.

Husbands and wives should share their thinking with one another. If you think your spouse won't understand, give him or her a chance to misunderstand before you judge. You may find out your spouse not only understands, but he or she can add in ways you never even thought of. Give credit where credit is due.

There are people who are interested only in sexual conquests, under the guise of marriage. If it's your karma to be involved in that type of action, you are going to go into it even though you'd rather do something else. If you do find yourself entering into marriage primarily for the sexual experience, then at least enjoy yourself. That may be all you're going to get out of it. The other person may just be there to enjoy himself, too—and then you'll both be going on to someone else. Enjoy yourself. Live right now. Take whatever happiness comes your way. If just a moment of happiness comes across your path in this world, take it. Don't abuse it. Don't misuse it. Take it and love it, and then let it go.

Getting married is nice, and sexual technique is nice. Really blending two consciousnesses together is fantastic. But after you're divorced, she may say, "He just thought he was a great lover. He wasn't; he was terrible." That's crucifixion. In spite of the truth, you may want to think you're entirely beautiful and good and wonderful and loving, and the divorce was all the other's fault.

A lot of people aren't happy in their marriage because they think their spouse is stepping out on them. The woman thinks, "My husband is probably going to go out and have sex with that pretty redhead down the street." So she hates that neighbor. The neighbor saves her child from drowning, however, pulling him out of the pool. Then the mother says, "Oh, my God, I hated you and now you've saved my child. What am I going to do?" Guilt is present at this point, so she says, "You can have my husband; it's okay. Anything, just to get rid of my guilt."

The other woman says, "I don't want your husband. I've never wanted your husband. I love my own and he loves me. What have you been thinking?" It's all been a fantasy.

So many times you fantasize and build things up in your mind that absolutely do not exist. There is no reality to match; there is nothing. This is like having sex with someone and envisioning that you're with somebody else. To me that is really prostitution because you're not here and now, experiencing what is. Enjoy the intimacies and the sacredness of life, right here, right now.

One good thing about sexual intercourse and the climaxing consciousness is that it does bring you *here* and *now*. All of a sudden all of your emotions and mind and everything is entirely present—if only for a few seconds. Instead of living that experience over and over, if you will just live "entirely present" all the time, right now, you will be in a state of ecstasy that will so transcend the sexual climax that sex will be a nothing to you; it may be a comedown.

As soon as you start the mind going through its analytical levels, you start splitting the consciousness. Then lust appears, and you start back in the treadmill of the rat going around the maze, seeking adventure, hoping to find something, wanting something, not that, not that, not that—*that!* But *that* wants somebody else, and you can't have *that,* and that's frustration. There's no cure for frustration, but there is a prevention: *Don't go into it.*

There is a song with lyrics that say, "I'm going to love more each day. I'm going to give more than I take. I'm going to live more for the sake of living love." When you do live love, everything becomes fantastic. You manifest here and now and receive God's grace. You bestow grace upon yourself from a higher consciousness. Then you are the Beloved. At that point, you don't need sex or marriage. In essence, you are married to everyone, to the whole world. It's all one thing, manifesting as different forms. You can look at some and love them, at others and love them, and at others and love them—and it's all the same love.

A day may come when you don't show love in the same way; it comes out of the heart. Then people say, "You don't look at me the same way you've looked at everybody else."

You say, "You're special."

They say, "I don't want the special; I want the regular." But when they look past the physical to the spiritual heart, they will see that the love is divine and present for all. If you let your "love" separate you, then it's not really love. If you sit home—separated and isolated—waiting for his phone call, that not love. In love, you're free. If you're home painting, busy, happy and fulfilled, and he calls, then that's wonderful. Your love and his love is matched.

Part of a marriage is taking the energies of both partners and putting them in one direction. Maybe the husband works so that his wife can stay home and take care of the children. Then it's a common goal of *both* the husband and wife to have beautiful, happy, intelligent children and to be financially stable at the same time. They both handle their part of the goal. It's not that *his* goal is to make money and *her* goal is to rear the children. They both share, and they become as one. If this idea becomes a barter system—"I'll take care of the kids if you give me a nice house" or "I'll give you my body if you give me money and possessions"—then it has become a form of prostitution. It is no longer a marriage, no longer love.

In a marriage, each one contributes one hundred percent. Then it doesn't matter who is fulfilling what role. If the goal is the same for both people, either partner may fulfill any part. Maybe the goal of the marriage is expression, and the life path of both the husband and wife is expression. If the husband's area of expression is art that is not lucrative financially, and the wife is working an $80,000 a year job as a fashion designer, then they're successful. It isn't just her success. It's *their* success—because they're together. Maybe a few years later she decides she wants to go back to school and learn something else, so she says, "Your turn, honey." Then he goes out and gets a financially successful job as a commercial artist so she can go to school. They are both sharing, cooperating, and supporting each other in their individual life patterns and in the marriage.

In a marriage, there is nothing to say that one role is necessarily "male" and one role is necessarily "female." There are common goals, and roles that support those goals. Either partner may fulfill any role. The roles may remain constant throughout a lifetime, or they may shift many times. It doesn't matter. As long as you give one hundred percent, then the marriage is complete and is working.

When you are married and are committed to the love you have for your spouse, then there is nothing you will not do. With that attitude, your lover is less likely to make demands upon you that will not be loving. So it's a two-way street. I was watching a television movie the other night where a man said to his girl, "If you get those people to move away from here, I'll marry you." That's suppression of the worst kind. That's emotional, psychic, and mental blackmail, not to mention sexual frustration. He dangled the carrot, and of course, she took it. So that made her a jackass. I'm sure a lot of women across the nation watched and said, "Don't do it; he's using you." But those same women may turn right around and let the man in their lives abuse and misuse them.

Do you know that married men rape their wives? They demand and force a sexual act, as if their wives were their property with which they could do anything they wanted. I'll bet there comes a day when a wife can take criminal action against her husband for that type of action. But I think perhaps she'd be further ahead to file for divorce long before that ever happens. It could not happen unless she were promoting it through her ignorance or fear. The husband promotes it through his misplaced "macho" consciousness.

To make a marriage work and endure is big business. It's one of the most full-time businesses around. It is one hundred percent. Even if you are out working another job one hundred percent, that marriage requires one hundred percent on top of that. You can never put your career, your occupation, your hobbies or anything else ahead of that loving consciousness present. There is nothing else more worthy than the loving consciousness. You throw all caution to the wind and love completely, unabashedly—everything. If you say to your husband, "I'm not going to do it that way," you shouldn't be married. If he says, "Hey, that's okay," then you *should* be married because he has the timeless understanding. Hold to him and say, "Anyway you want, honey. If you have all that understanding, wow, I'll try to match it." If you don't want to have sexual relations as often as your spouse does, ask yourself if you really love that person. If the answer is, "Yes, but I'm not going to do that!" then get divorced. You'll get divorced eventually, anyway, but it may be in ten years instead of now. And then you might have alimony, child support, and property settlements. Maybe you won't be able to afford it then. Get it over with today. End it. Get on with the spiritual upward flow of energy. Love God with all your heart, all your mind, and all your soul.

There may be a few men across the planet who are really great lovers, but most of them are lusters. However, lust can bring you your experience. I don't know if there can really be anything said about lust, except that it is. But if you keep your head and consciousness and attention on the areas of lust, you start collapsing inside. Then everyone you see becomes an object of sexual desire.

It's interesting to note than many men are really psychologically quite incapable. They really need the larger ego consciousness of a woman to prop them up, to make them feel worthwhile. Most women have larger egos than men. Because men often have the smaller ego, they die inside a lot. They spend a lot of time mentally speculating, "I wonder if I'm really worthy? I wonder if she really loves me?" One of the ways men feel they can prove themselves—and they have this in their consciousness as a habitual, addictive pattern—is, "If she will take me into her body, then she is demonstrating acceptance and understanding of me, and that means she loves me." It doesn't necessarily, but that is what the man thinks it means.

Many times when a man looks at a woman and thinks, "I sure would like to go to bed with her," he is really saying, "I feel so totally inadequate within myself that I can't hold up inside. I'm falling apart. Love me and then I will know that I am worthwhile." Of course, after he is through with his sexual climax and has the feeling of completion, he probably says, "Who needs you, you pig?" This is because his opinion of himself is low, and it follows "logically" that any girl in her right mind wouldn't have anything to do with him—because he's nothing. That really is a basic attitude of some men. It's a difficult one to have, because the man never really feels good about himself. It's a difficult attitude for the woman to handle because it makes her feel cheap and used. This type of man is often a smooth talker. He's got the line down real well. He can talk you right into bed, and then right out of bed as he goes on to the next conquest. Then you're upset and ask, "Why is he doing this to me?" He is only doing what you promote and what you allow. Why are *you* doing it?

Sometimes women get talked into bed because of their mothering instinct that says, "Oh, that little body. He's such a little boy, and I really love that quality. I'll do anything I can to help him feel better." He's not looking for a mother. He's looking for a lover. Make him stand up inside. If you're looking for a child, have your own or adopt one. Don't make your men into children.

Many people say, "There are so many roles I have to play in the family, so many hats I have to wear. How do I know the difference between a lust action towards the conjugal relationship and the spiritual action?" After sexual intercourse, if there is no love, no closeness, no oneness, no upliftment, no sharing—then it has been lust. You've lied if you've said otherwise. But if the relationship is spiritual, the love continues after the sexual action is finished.

A husband and wife have twin beds, and he wants to make love to her. So he says, "Honey, baby, why don't you come over here for a little while?" As she gets out of bed, she stubs her toe on the bedpost, and he says, "Oh, are you hurt, baby? Come here and let me make it better." But after sexual relations, she stubs her toe on the way back to her bed, and he says, "You clumsy idiot." His action has been one of lust, not love. If it's really love, it's love all the time—coming or going.

Love is not only the conjugal relationship. Love is all things. Love expresses on many levels. But love may certainly be expressed through the conjugal relationship. That's one way the soul makes love on the physical level. If the action is procreation, then it is, indeed, spiritual love. If the act is one of "I'll see you sometime..." then it names itself, and I don't have to. The soul responds to love. It rarely responds to anything else. It will not respond to the temporary "love" of a moment or two. But it will respond to an honest expression of love, because that is its nature—loving and happy and joyful.

Be honest in your family relationships. If someone does something you don't like—*tell them.* Don't say, "You don't cook like my mother used to cook." Your wife already knows that. Maybe you're fat and sloppy from your mother's cooking and she's trying to trim you down. If you don't want to be trimmed down, just tell her you're built for comfort, not for speed. Keep the humor in there, too.

When a couple gets mad at each other and she says, "I think you're stupid," he can say, "I think you're right." She may just crack up laughing. What else can she do? There's no more need to attack; she's already won. Then as she walks out the door, he can say, "And you're stuck with me."

She may say, "Yeah, and I'm so glad. And you're stuck with me."

He says, "That's just what I wanted all along." The fight's over—and they've both won.

If your spouse is starting to eat too much and is getting a little too fat, ask yourself what it is that you are not supplying that person. What nutrition (not food) are you leaving out of your diet with the person? Start talking. Get a

Husbands & Wives

dialogue going. He may say, "I don't know. I just feel like you don't love me."

She says, "I love you."

He says, "That's the word level."

She says, "What am I supposed to do? Hold you?"

He says, "That would be a start. Let's see if that will do it."

She says, "All right, I'll hold you."

He says, "But it feels like you're holding a wooden Indian or something." Don't patronize me. This isn't a platonic relationship."

She says, "Yes, it is."

If you have become platonic in your approach to your mate, then you are no longer married. You may live together until you die, but you are no longer married. Keep in mind that neither of you can take advantage of the other unless your spouse creates it, promotes it, or allows it. What does that mean? It means you're both on the same side.

When you start taking opposite sides, it becomes difficult to experience the oneness that is the consciousness and the best expression of marriage.

It's not childish or stupid to say, "I love you so much. You are so important to my life. You can do what you want to do; I'll still love you." If you think your wife would be out sleeping with every guy on the block if you said that, she may be anyway. If you go around to the next block, maybe you can get in line. Maybe you have not always shown her a loving consciousness. Maybe she is trying to teach you something. Or maybe she is just crying out to you, "Come love me. Come rescue me; get me out of this. Fulfill me. Let me know I'm worthwhile." Usually that's all it is.

People who are considering divorce have come to me after they've gone to their lawyers and the reconciliation judge and are still having trouble. I look at the husband and say, "Does it really bother you so much that she hangs nylons over the bathroom sink?"

He says, "Boy, that just really drives me up the wall."

I look at her and ask, "Does it really bother you that he throws his pants on the floor when he goes to bed?"

She says, "Yes, that just drives me crazy."

I say, "You both forget one thing—at one time her legs were in those nylons and his body was in those pants." They start thinking, "That's right." I say, "At one time that really turned you on."

She may say, "Yeah, but couldn't he just hang up his pants?"

I say, "Don't complain. That gives you a good excuse to go through his pockets for extra change before you hang them up."

She says, "Shh, he's not supposed to know I do that." It starts getting fun.

Husbands & Wives

He says, "Here I am, married to a spendthrift."

She says, "But you're such a pinchpenny...." And then they start fighting a little bit, which is nice because at least they're communicating.

Communication is probably one of the most important elements of marriage and family relations—simple *communication*. If something's bothering you, talk about it. I ask the husband, "Is it possible to hang up your pants?"

He says, "Sure."

I ask the wife, "Is it possible to hang your nylons someplace else?"

She says, "Sure."

Then I ask, "Why are you getting a divorce?"

She says, "I didn't think he cared—the way he nitpicked at me over my stockings."

I tell her, "He didn't pick at *you*. He picked at the way you hung up your stockings. You had yourself falsely identified with the stockings. You are not your stockings."

She says, "When he ripped them up and threw them out, it really burned me up."

I ask, "What did you do about that?"

She says, "I got some new ones."

I say, "Don't complain, now you're ahead."

He says, "I didn't know you got new stockings. Then I should get new pants." When a husband and wife start keeping score and trying to get even, the marriage may be in some trouble. You can't get even physically, emotionally or mentally. Spiritually you are already even, and that level encompasses all the others. If lovers and husbands and wives and children love each other spiritually, the rest of their lives will be beautiful.

Some people get married and spend the rest of their lives wondering why they did that. Forget it. You're never going to figure out that one. If you must waste your time, try to figure out who God is. When you figure that out, you'll know why you married. You married because your lover was more clearly manifesting to you your own radiant form of God. When your lover starts clouding that up is when you start yelling and pushing, trying to make that one let go of it again—"Let go. Show me that God-form again."

It's interesting that all the haranguing you place against your mate is trying to make that one release the energy form of pure love you first saw in that person and thought you couldn't live without. Later, you're trying to get away from the marriage. This is the contradictory field of energy in which we humans sometimes function. It's like, "Get away closer," or "Gee, that hurts good." The other person is sitting there, thinking, "What can I do?" Often the best thing to do is nothing; just let the person have fun in the confusion. There *is* something positive to be said about confusion; it is an indicator of energy moving through your consciousness. You should be thankful that you have that energy. If you don't know which way to turn, just let God turn you. Don't ask questions or you'll increase your confusion.

When you find that the one you love and are married to will not change to suit your whim or desire, you may move into a consciousness of pettiness and bickering. There is the love of getting along, the love of sharing, the love of compromising—to assist the greater relationship. But if, in compromising, you bemoan the results and feel great stress within yourself for "giving in," then your approach has been negative and does not reflect love. You say, "I did this for you; what are you going to do for me?" This is barter, not love. When people ask this of me, I say, "I will do nothing for you."

Through your actions, you ask people, "Will you allow me to love you?" You ask it in many ways, but one big way is, "Will you love me back?" So when the other person does not give love back, you fight and yell. You feel pettiness and hatred and betrayal within yourself, and you project it out to the other person. You are really just crying out, "Please help me. I need love." You *do* need love. You need it because it is part of your beingness to be fulfilled with love. But you can never be fulfilled through physical love. Physical love often brings sorrow. Emotional love often brings upset. Mental love often brings prejudice. But spiritual love brings the consciousness of God and the realization that all things are functioning in accordance with the one law which is God.

The thing you see in people that attracts you to them is love. It is Spirit. You are attracted to them because you want more of that. Once many years ago, I was visiting some very dear friends. As I walked up to their front door, I heard tremendous voices coming out of the "depths of hell." As they opened the door, I realized that it was those two yelling at each other. One of them hollered, "Come in and sit down!"

I said, "Don't yell at me. I'm not married to you."

The wife turned around and said, "Well, if you were, I'd be better off."

I said, "Now, you've just ruined my friendship with your husband..."

He said, "No, if she wants you, she's welcome to you."

I said, "Now you are ruining my friendship with your wife because I couldn't measure up to the way you love her."

He said, "What!?"

I said, "I couldn't measure up to the way you love her."

He said, "How do you know?"

I said, "You two chose each other. I've been an outsider from the very beginning. You're the one she loves, not me, not anyone else. Just you."

He said, "Well, if she loves me so much, why does she yell at me?"

I said, "Answer that yourself."

He said, "She's trying to get rid of me; she's trying to drive me crazy."

I said, "That would only be a putt; you're almost crazy now."

He said, "I think maybe she wants a divorce."

I asked her, "Do you?"

She said, "No."

I said, "So why does she yell at you? What does she want?"

He said, "She wants me to do this and that, and she wants to supervise."

I said, "Why?"

He said, "What are you doing, anyway? Marriage counseling?"

I said, "Obviously! Why else would I be here? I'm doing a marriage counseling, and you two pay attention so when you get the bill you'll think it was worth it."

They said, "You'd charge us?"

I said, "Sure. You take it out on each other. Why shouldn't I?"

They knew I was winning. I said to her, "If you want to yell at him, then yell that you hope he breaks his neck—and mean it."

She said, "That's terrible; I couldn't say that."

I said, "How about just telling him to go to hell."

She said, "No, I don't want to say that to him."

I said, "Then tell him to go to heaven."

She said, "He isn't worthy of it."

I said, "What do you have to do to be worthy?"

She looked at me and said, "Can I talk to you by yourself for a minute?"

I looked at him and asked, "Can I?"

He said, "I don't care what you do."

I said, "You don't? Okay, I'll go in the bedroom and talk."

He said, "No, talk over there in my study."

I said, "Oh, you *do* care?"

He said, "Sure, I care."

She said, "You care? That was all I was yelling about. I just wanted to know if you cared."

He said, *"Really?* You mean these last few years of us verbally getting divorced and married and divorced and married was just you telling me how you love me?"

She said, "That's not *how* I love you. I was trying to tell you to get closer so I *could* love you. But you are always doing other things. I can't get through to you unless I yell, and then you always yell back."

He said, "Yelling at me is love?"

She said, "Sort of. It's a sign of love."

He said, "Well, you don't have to yell at me."

She looked at me and asked, "Will you go home?" I was already on my way out the door.

These are dear people; they were sure being rough on each other, however—far, far too rough. Now their family is nearly grown. Their marriage is a good one; they still yell at each other, however. It's okay. Now they both know that's part of their love.

Perhaps it's ideal to have a family consisting of a husband and wife and their children, the husband being the high priest and the wife being the high priestess of the family. If the father gives up his position, however, and will not bring spiritual leadership into the family, then it is up to the mother to handle that position. He might say, "But I bring the paycheck home all the time." That's appreciated, but unfortunately that doesn't bring the Spirit of love into the family. It is true that if the father doesn't do it, the mother must. If the mother won't, then the children must. I have taught children what I call the "nine magic words" that are available to them—and to everyone. The first three are "I love you;" the second three are "God bless you," and the third three are, "Peace, be still." These words are powerful.

I knew a young man once whose parents fought a good deal. It disturbed him tremendously when they fought. So I told him of a technique to use the next time they fought. It was to mentally say to them over and over in his mind, "I love you. God bless you. I love you. God bless you." He tried it the next time they got into a fight. He stayed in the next room and just kept projecting those thoughts to them. It was only a matter of minutes before they were laughing and kidding around as they finished up the dinner dishes together. The change was really a dramatic one.

These words will work. You don't always have to be silent about it, either. If you are feeling a special love for your spouse or your children or your parents, these words are often the nicest things in the world to say. They only take a second; they can change the world.

There is nothing quite so nice as when you are in bed at night and your husband scratches your head and rubs your ears, or when your wife massages your back and neck. It's just these little tiny things that make the whole marriage and the whole love affair. It makes everything all right when you come in the door and your wife lights up and says, "Wow, I'm so glad to see you. I'm really happy you're home."

Later on, she can share the disturbances and the troubles. *Later on.* Not right away. If you come in the door and she hits you with what the kids have done and what went wrong with the washer, she may find you coming home later and later.

It works the other way, too. If she comes home and you start berating her—"Where were you? Why are you getting home this late?"—she may fire back, "What do you care where I was?" Then the fight's on. When she walks in that door, it doesn't matter where she's been. She's home now. Love her. Seduce her. Do whatever you do that brings the two of you into a oneness. If you really do it right, she'll never go very far. You won't have to worry, and you won't have regrets that you didn't give her your best. It can be simple. It's often in the little things, the little ways that you give her your attention and let her know you care. This works both ways, so whether you are a man or a woman, take these things to heart, and take care of those you love.

Chapter 2

and Kids

It's very important to have love in the family. The family is the foundation of society. Love is the foundation of the family. God is the foundation of love. This love isn't the love of "Now do what I want you to do or I won't believe you love me." It's the love of, "Whatever you do, I love you." This is pure love. It can't just be stated; that's lip service. You have to *demonstrate* that love, *every* day—in ways you never dreamed of. People sometimes speak with words as though they're close to God, even though their hearts may be far away from God. It is where the heart is that matters.

When Jesus said that one must be childlike to enter into the Kingdom of Heaven, I think he was saying that a person must be loving and innocent and open—which are qualities of children. Often when I look into children's eyes and into their consciousnesses, one of the first things I see there *is trust.* They come into this world completely at the mercy of the world. The soul consciousness places itself in a very restricted form that has very little ability. It really can't take care of itself at all. It has to have everything done for it until it can learn to do things for itself. This is a process of training the body to do what the soul can use it to do. So the soul comes into the physical body with this perfect trust and says, "Here I am. I can't do one thing for myself." It doesn't even say, "I trust you to do it." It just demonstrates that trust by being here. It really is perfect trust.

As children grow, they continually demonstrate their trust. They come up to their mother or father to ask questions, and they really want to know the answers. They come in perfect acceptance that they are going to be told the truth. So don't ever lie to your children. If you do, you forfeit the greatest trust that these youngsters have. If they can't trust their parents, who can they trust? Where can they turn if they can't turn to their mothers and fathers to get the answers they need for their lives? Parents say, "But what if they ask me about sex?" If your kids ask that type of question, they are apparently ready for the answer. You have to listen very carefully to what they are really asking you, however, and just answer the question. Nothing more. If they want more information, they'll ask.

There is a story of a boy who asks his mom, "Where did I come from?"

She says, "Ask your Dad."

So he says, "Daddy, where did I come from?"

And Kids

Dad says, "Uh...the doctor brought you in his little black bag."

The boy says, "Come on, Daddy, where did I come from?"

He says, "The stork brought you."

The kid says, "Daddy, where did I come from?"

He says, "Well, I'll tell you...." So he explains in great detail how children are conceived and how they come through the mother's body out into the world."

When he is finished, the kid just looks at him and says in bewilderment, "Jimmy, next door, said he came from Boston. I just wanted to know where I came from." You have to really find out what children are asking so that you don't get caught up in a bunch of miscellaneous information that doesn't answer what the child is asking.

When the time comes that your children do ask where they came from and how they were born, explain it to them

And Kids

in a very matter-of-fact way—as if you were explaining how to play a guitar. Explain it in a loving way. You might want to have a book present to show the body and how the baby grows within the mother. If you don't tell your children the facts of life, they'll find out from someone else, behind a barn or in back of a playground or somewhere. If you betray their trust by not answering their questions honestly, they'll never come to you for the big, important questions later on. If you teach them honestly and openly, they'll keep giving you the opportunity to teach them. Then they won't have to learn all the misinformation from their friends or sneak books into their rooms to try to find out what the story is.

Youngsters have not conditioned their emotions or their minds to fear the world. They're very much in love with the world. They are very much in love with their parents. They also have a little "animal" consciousness within them, and that "animal" consciousness says, "Feed me right now; gimme that; don't do that." I call this part the basic self. That is the part you have to educate. I'm not talking about training; you can train a dog. I'm talking about *educating*. You take the time to explain to the youngster what you are doing and why you are doing it.

I've heard parents say, "Educating a child takes too long." You have a Christ present in that child. Can't you take a little time with it? What if your child asks you a question and you say, "I don't have time—go out and play," and he runs out in the street and is hit by a car? Then you think, "Oh, my God, I had all the time in the world. Why didn't I take it?" Never, never place yourself in a position where you will have bad feelings if the results of your action are negative. That hurts and hurts and hurts; even while you sleep, it hurts. Always keep yourself clear by doing the very best you can—all the time. It's not necessarily easy. It's a twenty-five hour a day job.

When children come up and tug on you and say, "Mommy....Mommy...." they want something. Even if you're busy, take the time to see if they need anything. If you're with friends, they will understand that you must take a moment for your child. If they don't understand, they are not your friends. Don't worry about them, and take a moment for your child. You don't have to interrupt your conversation with friends for fifteen minutes while you talk to your child; just take a few seconds to find out what is needed.

When children need something, they come to you to fulfill their prayers. And they really are issuing prayers.

And Kids

They are depending upon you to see what you can do to fulfill them. Sometimes children are just after love. Don't be afraid to pick them up, cuddle them, love them, rub their backs, and kiss and hug them. It's neat to demonstrate that kind of affection. And it's fun. Give them all the love you can muster, and they will return it to you in more ways than you can imagine. They'll do little things—like come running up to you and put their arms around you and say, "I love you, Daddy," or "I love you, Mommy." They'll give you a great big kiss and then turn around and run out to play, leaving you completely devastated. They come out of nowhere with this bountiful joy of childhood and give it to you. That is the kingdom of heaven.

In the kingdom of heaven, there is just love. It's bountiful. It's there for no reason. You don't have to earn love. If you let it, this love will just flow from your children. When your children get older, however, you have to earn their respect. That is something that you don't get for free just because you're a mother or father. You *earn* their respect. You have to continually do things in such a way that your youngsters can look up to you and say, "That's my Dad. That's my Mom. I love them. They don't lie to me. I can trust them. They tell me the truth." Then when the rest of the world is gossiping and bad-mouthing one another, your children will be able to stand up and say, "I don't have to be a part of this, because I'm already a part of a group—a group that is called family. *And I don't betray my family.*"

A child has a basic self within the consciousness structure, just as adults do. The basic self is like a little "animal" consciousness within the child's consciousness. Sometimes that little basic has trouble with this world. It's very young, and it is just learning. As a parent, you can work directly and specifically with your child's basic self.

If you have put your child to bed for the night, take a few moments for "we" time, just between you and your child. This is one way that you can work with your child's basic self. It's not the quantity of time, it's the quality that's important. As you take time to talk to your child, ask questions about the day. The child is probably getting into the twilight area of not being fully awake anymore, knowing that it's time to go to sleep. As the child's consciousness drops away, you'll be communicating with the basic self. Ask, "Did you have a good day?" If the child says yes, ask, "What did you do today that you'd like to do again tomorrow?" The child will tell you. Then you can ask, "What did you do today that you wouldn't want to do tomorrow?" The child will tell you.

And Kids

If you ask if it was a good day and the child says no, you can still follow with the same questions; you're not really concerned with the answer to the original question. You're just getting the child to tell you what's going on and giving the child the opportunity to share his or her beingness with you. There won't be any generation gaps with this approach.

When you ask your child how their day went, suppose their answer is, "I didn't like it when Susie played with my toy."

Ask the child, "How do you think you would solve that tomorrow?" You will get the youngster to sort of reflect and think about it instead of just reacting to his or her emotions.

The child may say, "I'm too tired to answer."

You say, "Okay, go to sleep now. In the morning you can wake up with the answer and, if you like, you can tell me about it." Then remember to ask about it the next morning. See what the child says. The next night ask, "How did you handle Susie and the toy?"

The child may say, "It never came up today."

Ask, "How would you handle it if it did come up?" This prepares the youngster for future situations. It's like a rehearsal of how to handle situations. Maybe when the child sees Susie coming, he or she can just put the toy away because Susie doesn't know how to play with it. That's fine because it's the child's toy which the child has a right to protect. Or maybe the youngster can teach Susie to play with it so she won't break it; that's fine because there is the right to do that. It becomes easy.

As your child is dropping off to sleep, that's a good time to clear any irritation or disturbance *you've* had with the child. You can sit beside the bed after the child has fallen asleep and call the basic self forward; it will come to you. You might imagine that the basic comes and sits on your lap. How do you know if it's really there? You don't care. It may seem like it's all your imagination, when you start getting results, however, you'll know that there's a reality to it. Tell the basic self that everything is okay, that you love it very much. Tell it, "You're going to grow up fine. I love you and support you." Then let the basic self go back to the body to maintain it. This may take only a few seconds. These levels of the basic self are very real. That little basic may feel very threatened and very frightened of this world. Reassure it that everything's okay, that you love it, and that you will take care of it.

If you're going through a divorce or a difficult time with your spouse, you might want to take some extra time to reassure your children's basic selves that you love them and are not abandoning them. Let them know that the love is still constant, even if the outer situation is changing. Let them know they'll be taken care of, that they will not be hurt or harmed. Children need love, and they need to be able to trust you. You're all they've got. They depend on you for just about everything. *Don't let them down.*

In the first two years, children learn more complex behavior patterns than at any other two-year period in their lives. They learn to walk, talk, think, follow directions, remember, and coordinate and move the body so it can do what they want it to do. The first two years or so are extremely important. Children learn best through love. When they love something, they look forward to it and are wide open to the energy of information. That's why you should prepare a loving place for children to come into—so that they can be open to receive the goodness that you have in your heart for them.

Have you ever stopped to think why teacher's pets get good grades? The youngster who is the teacher's pet loves the teacher, loves the subject, and is learning it so fast that he can't help but get good grades. I used to tell my young students, "If you want to get good grades in my class, become the teacher's pet. The teacher's pet has assignments in on time, passes every test, and has a good attitude."

These kids would say, "That could be anybody!"

I said, "Sure, and in here, that's the teacher's pet. And if you're not doing that, you'll not be this teacher's pet. Then you might not have the experiences you want to have." I had whole

And Kids

classes full of teacher's pets. Any one of them could come up and sit by my desk at any time because they were all my "pets." They could ask me questions about anything, and I'd sit and look at the situation with them. I'd rarely tell them the answer; I'd help them think it through, however, and find their own answers, solve their own problems.

A big part of schooling is learning to think and solve problems. Then that ability can be taken into the world and used with whatever comes the youngster's way. That's the value of education—to give children an ability to creatively solve problems. Then they can apply that ability to anything. They may forget the information; they'll always be able to look that up, however. They won't forget the process of thinking and problem-solving if they have learned it in an atmosphere of love and support. They will have confidence and

And Kids

joy and love as the foundation for their lives. This golden age is going to be an age of love; so if you can foster this childlike attitude of openness in your children toward you as parents and toward the teacher, the pastor, the policeman, and so forth, you will be creating the golden age for yourself and your kids.

When youngsters go to their schools, they are not there to be berated or picked on or shown their stupidity. They probably already know that. They are probably already afraid that their ignorance is going to be demonstrated to them. The teacher is there to give *success* to the children, just as the parents are supposed to give success to them. Of course, they should be disciplined. Your job as educators, whether you're a parent or a teacher or both, is to give the children enough information of the same type that other children are getting so that they can compete with their peers. That's education as it is today. A lot of young people are dropping out of school, thinking that if that's all it is, who needs it? Yet, if they are to compete successfully, they need it.

Make sure that you explain to your kids that school tests do not record their failure. The tests record the area of their weakness and point up where a little extra work is necessary. It reveals to them their lack and points up their strengths. Teach your children to never be fearful of tests, but to welcome them—any test, any time. When you don't have a test, you wonder how you're doing, and you don't have any reference points to let you know.

I used to ask my classes if they wanted one test at the end of the semester or a lot of tests regularly through the semester that could be averaged at the end. If they were smart, they always chose "lots of tests." That way, if they failed one, they could study harder and make good grades on the others. They knew if the teacher gave a lot of tests, they could figure out what areas he tested and know what to study to come out with high grades. They'd be able to "psyche the teacher out." If there were just one test at the end, however, it might be too late for them to gather the energy to pass.

When a teacher gives many tests as time goes along, students can prepare as they go along. Then one failure is no problem. It means that they have to learn that information better because questions about it will reappear later in an accumulative test. That's life. Life does *exactly* the same thing. Sometimes it's called the "university of hard knocks." It is true that the lessons you "fail" in life will come around again. You'll get another opportunity to see if you learned. When you do learn to pass a test, you will have achieved mastery of that area and may no longer be tested on that.

Many youngsters today are the bridge from the old age into the new age, the new consciousness. So you teach them the information they will need to be successful. Give it to them really well. If your children are having trouble remembering their school lessons or what you tell them to do, you can help them increase their awareness and concentration. When you tell them something, just tell them a little bit at a time, and then ask them to repeat it back to you. Don't just ask them if they understood because they'll probably say they do, whether they do or not. If they have to repeat it back to you, you'll know they heard, and it will help "set" it in their memory. You can use this technique in many situations. You may want to take their faces in your hands and turn their heads so they're looking directly at you. Then tell them what you want them to know and have them repeat it to you. When you help your children with their homework, have them respond verbally and often to you. Ask a lot of questions and make sure they can answer them. Make their education an active process, not a passive one. Make sure they are active in *their* participation. That's the way they'll learn.

Once a child is school age, it's good to keep yourself aware of and informed about when there are tests and what homework assignments are due on what days. Then you can make sure the child is prepared. Unprepared homework assignments are a great cause of illness among kids. If your little ones seem to be falling into this pattern, one thing you can tell them is, "Your stomach probably won't hurt if you do what's right. It's often when you do what's wrong that your stomach hurts." The basic self and the area of the emotions reside in the stomach chakra. So it's very true that if the emotions are upset or the basic self is in rebellion, the child's stomach will tend to be upset.

Some children learn to use illness to get attention, or they'll learn to use it as blackmail to get what they want. You have to be careful here to keep in mind that the illness might be real; so you always check it out. Take the child's temperature. See if an imbalance shows up there. One good way to see if the child is "faking" or not is to set up some guidelines that say, "If you're too sick to go to school today, then you're too sick to go to the game (or whatever it is that they are looking forward to) tonight." It can be amazing how fast things clear up.

When children are interested in something, they can really become

And Kids

enthusiastic about it and start jumping and running around—and you can get really excited with them and want to get involved in their enthusiasm and their love. When they play, they don't want to play with somebody who is conditioned and restricted; they want somebody who is free, someone who can play the imagination game with them. They don't know that adults are all playing imagination games, too. Adults have just "sophisticated" their games and call them "fantasies."

Children's games are make-believe. They're honest. I often think their games are better and more honest than adult's. Children have the flexibility to drop their games and go on to something else, instantly. Adults who fantasize seem to get caught up in their fantasies and project them onto everybody they see. That can become difficult. That is childish, not childlike.

And Kids

Your children will tend to cope with the world much the same way you do. Children learn by example. If you don't do too well, how are they going to do better? If you're really good at lifemanship, however, they're going to learn. Take your children out into the world and teach them what to do. Take them to social gatherings, churches, bowling alleys, circuses, art galleries, parades, and the theater. Show them how to behave by demonstrating how to behave. Explain to them the differences in different activities.

Children are eternally curious. I'm sure you've all had the experience of answering children's questions and then being asked, "Why?" You explain, and they say, "Why?" They want to know how it works and how they can work it. That's what they want to know. They're really saying, "Give it to me so I can see what it is."

And Kids

One day a young couple was at my home, and they had their little daughter with them. She asked for a drink of water, and when her Dad got her one, she asked where the water came from. He told her it came from the faucet in the sink. She said. "Why?" He said it came through the pipes under the house. She said, "Why?" He said that the city provided water for people who lived there. She said, "Why?' I came along about this time, picked her up, took her over to the sink, showed her the faucet and how to turn it on, and let her fill every nearby glass, bowl and cup with water. That was what she wanted. She wanted to know how *she* could do it, what that process was. Words weren't going to satisfy her. She needed the experience.

Take time to work with children. They have a consciousness that is open to learning. Show them how things

And Kids

work. Let them *do* things. Give them some information, show them something, and then let them do it. Have them play information back to you immediately. That's a test to see if they got it. When you do it that way, you don't set up the obstacle of, "There will be a test on Friday." There are tests on Monday, Tuesday, Wednesday, Thursday, Friday, Saturday and Sunday. Testing is a continuous state of revealing yourself to yourself.

When you become a so-called "adult," you often feel like the world didn't give you a chance. It's never given anybody a chance. The world is to be reached into and used. You can't take it because it's not yours; you can use it, however. Things of this world are to be used. If you have something that you can't use, pass it along to someone who can. If everyone did this, do you think there would be shortages in this world?

And Kids

When you teach your children to face the world and the people in it with honesty and truth, you are giving them a most valuable key for living. A while ago I was coming into the United States from Mexico, and as we came up to the border station, the customs man seemed very uptight as he began asking us the routine questions. So I asked him, "Are you angry with us?" The question completely disarmed him.

He said, "No, of course not," and then he didn't know what to do next. So he said, "Let this man over here talk to you." We pulled the car over and another customs man came up, asked us a question or two which we answered, and said, "Okay, good-bye." There was nothing to hide; we were functioning in honesty and trust. To state it as openly as we did was quite a surprise to the border patrolman. When you hide something, then you are not functioning in honesty, and you will not have love. When you are open, saying, "You can see everything that is going on," then there is nothing hidden. All is present. That is a very easy way to live and to teach your children to live.

Remember that there is an innocence, openness, and trust in children that manifests as freedom. If you are going to do something in your home that you don't want the neighbors and everybody else in the world to know about, don't do it in front of your children. They probably don't know a restrictive consciousness, and they'll tell everybody just about everything. Anything you want others to know or don't care if they know, you can do in front of your child. A child communicates its love by information, by talking about the things that are close to it. And one of the things closest to a child is the father and mother and the things they

And Kids

do. So they'll tell the neighbors all about you. You'd better live in the way you want it reported to the world. Live what you want the kids to tell the neighbors, and you'll be in good territory.

When there is more than one child in the family, there will most likely be some times of friction between the children. If one of them comes to you and says, "My sister did this" or "My brother did that"—that is only one child's point of view of what the other one did. Children are often brought together in family patterns to sandpaper each other and to teach each other. Your job is to see that no one gets hurt and that no one exerts an overpowering type of infliction against the other. Other than that, your attitude can be that they will learn from one another.

Kids, in their actions, teach each other to withstand the world. The play they go through teaches them how to win and lose both inside and outside. If they play a game and lose and become so frustrated that they have a temper tantrum or have to go to their room, they may not be learning. When they can say, "It was just a game," and go on to the next thing, then they're learning. If they can let the other children win, then they walk away winners, too. This is cooperation and flexibility.

Children have to be taught to laugh at themselves and not to live their lives according to the opinions of others. Teach them to play roles and have fun with it. Let them dress up in funny costumes and have a good laugh at themselves. Let them put on plays and act out their ideas. These things are really healthy. It's important that children play. They learn many necessary things through their play.

If one sister or brother is purposefully teasing or annoying another, teach

And Kids

the other that he or she does not have to allow that. Teach the child that it is possible to walk away from the situation and go somewhere else. We do this as adults. If we are in an irritating situation, we can ask others to change their approach. We can tell them we don't like their expression, and why. And if that doesn't work, we can either put up with it or leave. Teach your children the same choices.

Sometimes children let their imaginations run away with them. They "see" all sorts of frightening things in their imagination and then carry the fear out into this existence. Then you may have screaming children on your hands for no apparent reason. Explain to them how the imagination works. Explain to them that they create these pictures and images, and that they can create happy pictures if they want. Play imagination games with them. Teach them how to imagine beautiful things. Teach them how to change scary images into funny ones. If they see a monster chasing them, teach them to alter that monster into a very tiny monster and see him running off a cliff while they stand safely behind a tree and watch. It's easy to teach them to change these images.

If something happens to your child that is physically frightening or upsetting, teach the child to work with the imagination to change the image. If the youngster sees the family dog get hit by a car, take some time to sit with the child, and give him or her the image of the dog running safely past the car down the street. Consciously the child will know that the dog was hit; the basic self will release that "horror picture" of the dog being hit, however, and the child will feel better.

Teach your children to envision their own success and happiness. If they have tests coming up in school, teach them to creatively see themselves taking the tests and passing them. Don't forget to make sure they study, too. It's important that they see themselves being successful. Make it a game. Keep their attitude positive. Keep their spirits up and bright and active.

Teach your children three things. First, teach them that the rhythm of what they are doing can be their own rhythm when they are alone and when they are with others, they must fit with the rhythm of the group. Teach them the rhythm. See how they fit in. Then teach them harmony: not to be louder than others or off-key, how to blend with the group. Teach them to make their consciousnesses an addition to the group, not an irritation.

Second, teach your children flexibility. If things don't go their way, then the children go the way it's happening.

And Kids

Teach them to move to what is going on, to pick up new rhythms and make new harmonies. You teach them these things at home, using games. You play games with them. They play one of your games, then you play one of their games. Give them this idea of give and take. When they get out in the world with other kids and want to play certain games, and the other kids say no, your children will be able to agree to play other games. When those games are over, they'll be able to say, "Now, let's play this," and the other youngsters will probably agree. They'll want a new game, and your child will have lots of experiences in creating games—and he or she will be successful. In teaching flexibility, you teach your children how to win and lose. When they really know how to lose a game gracefully, they'll always be winners. Losing one game won't destroy their confidence or self-

And Kids

esteem. They'll handle it and go on to the next thing.

Third, teach your children to use what they can use, and to allow other kids to use what they can't. Let them play with a toy for as long as their interest holds. Don't let them "hoard" a lot of toys at the same time, because they can't play with them all at once. Let them play with one toy at a time. When they finish with that toy, teach them to exchange it for another. That teaches them not to get spread out too thin in the world, not to get involved with too many things.

Youngsters sometimes get spread too thin in their social activities very early in life. Then you'll find that they're afraid to go to school because they don't have their homework done. If you ask them about it, they'll say, "By the time I got through with sports and leadership training and dance lessons and choir practice, there was no time to do my homework." They have some choices. They need to cut out something. You, as a parent, must see to it that they take the time to complete their educational pattern, because through that they will be taught the information necessary to compete with other people. They must learn the information well and accurately, because this is what society is moving upon. And if you go counter-society or revolutionary, you'll fail miserably. So you teach them within the system, and then you teach them to evolve the system. Through evolution, they can bring about the change that is needed. It can come as a very smooth, upward swing. Revolution means to rebel and destroy, rebel and destroy, rebel and destroy. It's a self-perpetuating cycle of destruction. Evolution, on the other hand, is peaceful, constructive change.

And Kids

When you teach children, teach them in the consciousness of their experience. Use their language to talk to them. If it's baby-talk, you use baby-talk. If it's love-talk, you use love-talk. It should *all* be love-talk. Even when you are saying, "Shh, be quiet," the child should not hear any harshness. The child should hear, "I love you very much; please be quiet now." Then the youngster will be quiet just to please you.

Teach children that their work is their love made manifest. Let them know that there are a lot of ways to demonstrate love. They can't always be hugging and kissing everyone to show their love. Teach them that things like doing their homework and helping around the house are also demonstrations of their love. Teach them to go within to their inner kingdom of heaven and awaken their inner strength—then to take that strength into the world to accomplish.

And Kids

If you have children or are planning to have children, give them everything you've got. You will never be depleted or tired if you give them all you have with *love*. If you just give a little bit, you'll get weary. Give your children everything you can; support them totally, and you'll never be tired. You'll be filled with the love of Spirit and the energy of that love as you go along.

Chapter 3

Love

&

Discipline

Discipline is the prelude to freedom. Therefore we enter willingly into discipline to gain freedom. Remember those multiplication tables you learned in school? Maybe you struggled to learn them; once you did, however, you could do them anytime you wanted. When you got older, you realized that the discipline of math gave you freedom. There were shortcuts; things were faster. You could arrive at solutions and answers and definitive processes rapidly. It took hours and hours of "3 x 3 = what?" It took great effort to bring yourself into that type of discipline, and you probably had a mother and father plus a teacher that you "hated" because they were working for your freedom by giving you the necessary discipline of the world. They taught you to overcome, to stay in a consciousness of relative freedom until you entered into another, higher discipline. When you forget the rungs of the ladder by which you move up into Spirit is when you start to descend by that very same ladder.

One of the nicest experiences you can have is when you wake up and realize that each day is the day that God has prepared for you. You just run over with love inside of you for everything around. You look at your children and know so much love. You look at the toys at the top of the stairs, and instead of tripping and falling on them, or even making a point of it, you just pick the toys up and place them where they belong. Then, through your love, you teach your children the discipline of responsibility to themselves and to others in this physical world.

Love & Discipline

Young children have some of the most beautiful qualities, and one of them is their pure faith—not faith as a word, but as a demonstration. Their faith says that those people who are their mother and father are going to have the necessary discipline to take care of them in the midst of all their messing up (and they do mess up a lot of things). They *know* their folks will take care of it all. It is tremendous to support your child in that type of faith and to demonstrate love through it all. If your action is one of living love, the basis of perfect faith, then you can look forward to the sun coming up tomorrow in your consciousness as well as in the world. You will joyfully do those things that tomorrow brings to you.

Babies are so close to the consciousness of God that the mere essence of Light radiating from them makes you, as a parent, take care of them—almost whether you like it or not. When you see their Light, there's practically no way that you cannot take care of your children. When they look up to you and are crying, you do everything in the world to help them. Often, you are just trying to shut them up, which is not necessarily the best approach. When babies cry, check to see if anything is wrong. Check to see if they're hungry or wet or tired or whether their clothes are binding them. If everything's okay and they keep crying, let them cry. It's all right. Maybe they're just exercising their lungs. Check it out every time—3 a.m., 4 a.m.—it doesn't matter. If they cry, get up and check. The time you're too lazy to check is the time that something could be seriously wrong. And if something happens to your child as a result of your neglect, that's a very heavy burden. So discipline yourself to get up and check. The time you don't is the time you're going to think, "Oh, my God, why didn't I check?" Then you go through your own personal hell. There are enough hells on the planet without setting one up for yourself out of neglect and irresponsibility. Take care of the children. Do everything for them with the most perfect love and support that you have within you.

You should love your children equally when they are good and when they are bad—so that they know your love is always there. When the children are bad, change their frequency by envisioning the positive. They will grasp the new image and move to the positive faster than you can imagine. If you bend them into submission, however, they will wait for a chance to get back at you. Right in the middle of the night, they'll holler, "I need a drink of water." So you get up and get the water, and then they wet the bed so you have to get up again and change it. They may do that night after night after night. Consciously they probably don't know that they're doing this to get back at you; there are many levels of consciousness below the conscious, however. Wetting the bed is often the way they let you know they are dissatisfied with the way things are functioning and that they need more attention and love.

When kids feel they're not getting the love and attention to which they're entitled, they may go to all sorts of extremes to get what they want from you. This can take a lot of forms. One way is the temper tantrum. A way to stop children from crying and screaming and throwing real temper tantrums is to lay on the floor beside them and do it just as loud or louder. They'll stop and look at you. They'll see what they look like, and it will sort of embarrass them. They'll think, "Wow, that's strange." If they realize that you are doing this because they are doing it, they'll stay out of that area. This technique can bring change in other areas, too. If your kids are doing something that is irritating you, get in there with them and run the response out to some ridiculous extreme. Although you may have to go a long way, you'll stop the response.

One day I happened to appear on the scene when a young mother I know was feeding her child. The little girl was into the experience of playing with her food and water. She was doing whatever she could to prolong the play, and she was driving her Mom up the wall. Mom was trying to make her stop and just eat; she wasn't going for it, however. I came along and saw what was happening and decided that I'd stop it once and for all. So I sat down with her, and together we explored all the many things you can do with your food. I showed her how to hold the water in her mouth and let just a little bit drool out one side and then the other. I showed her how to take the water and hold it between her lips and her teeth and then suck it back through her teeth—it makes a terrible noise. We tried blowing into the water glass. We tried all sorts of things for about a half an hour.

I finally got to the point where I told her to take the water in her mouth and then just let it all drool all over her chin, neck, dress, and everything. She looked at me very quietly and said, "No." That was the end of it. She hasn't done any of that since. We explored the area so completely that it was finished. It was pretty sloppy, but it was over in thirty minutes—not days and weeks of irritation and battling. This type of technique can be effective for working with the kids in certain areas.

When you are setting up household chores and are asking your children to be a part of this action, make sure they can do what you're asking them to do. Make sure they know what to do physically. If you're expecting them to make their beds, make sure that they know how to make the beds. Do it with them, show them, teach them. Make a game out of it. Make it fun. When they can handle that, let them know that you expect them to do that every day. Do this with all the chores. Then, if they don't do what they know they're expected to do, discipline is necessary.

A friend of mine was having trouble with her son not doing his chores. She'd tried everything she could imagine, and still no change. She'd talked to him and explained to him why he must do these things. She'd spanked him— no results. She'd sat him in the corner, and he'd spit on the wall. She finally told him that when he did his chores by a certain time, he could have a popsicle. Then, close to that time, she took the popsicle out of the freezer and put it on the sink. If he got the chores done in time, he got the popsicle. If he didn't, it melted. There were no second chances. The popsicle was gone forever if he didn't get those chores done. It worked. It's a good technique. Sometimes you have to be creative in your approach to discipline.

When children need discipline, it should be done immediately—they may not connect the incident with the punishment if there is a time gap. A child I know used to think that she could get away with a whole lot by making her demands public. Her folks would take her to a movie, and in the theater she would start yelling, "I WANT POPCORN. I WANT ICE CREAM. I WANT SODA POP." They would say, "No, we don't have enough money for that. We just have enough money for the show."

She'd yell, "I DON'T CARE. I WANT IT." Her folks wouldn't do too much because it was "embarrassing" to have to discipline your kid in a theater full of people. After one night of everyone in the theater complaining, however, they decided that they would talk about it. They knew that waiting until they got home to discipline her wasn't working. So they decided that the next time there was a disturbance, the discipline would be immediate; then the child would know what she was being disciplined about. The next time they went to the show and she started her disturbance, they took her out to the car and spanked her very firmly and said, "You *cannot do that.* We are going back into the show, and if you raise a disturbance again, you will be spanked in front of the whole group." She went in and sat down, and there was never a disturbance again. She knew that the discipline would happen rapidly. They didn't discipline her out of their anger; they disciplined her out of their love. They disciplined her so that she would learn proper behavior and be able to go to the movies with them rather than stay home with a babysitter. Parents really have tremendous responsibilities to their youngsters. The discipline is not for you, to make you happier or to make you feel better—it is for the children you love so much, so that they can fit better in the group action.

One way to handle children who are crying and fussing and not cooperating is to take them to their rooms and tell them they will stay there as long as they are crying and unhappy. Tell them that when they can be happy again, they can come out and join the family. Explain to them that their temper tantrums are inflictions on the rest of the family, and that they will be welcome when their attitudes are happy again. Let them know you love them, regardless; let them know that they cannot inflict themselves on their family and that their attitudes are what you are disciplining, not them. Let them have their favorite toys or some water—whatever they need. This isn't punishment; this is discipline.

If they come out of their rooms in three seconds and their attitudes have changed, that's great. If it takes them three hours to come into balance, that's fine, too. Check on them periodically. Make sure they're okay. Maybe you can play some music—whatever helps create a harmonious environment that helps to bring them back in balance. When they do come out, take the time to do something special with them—to reinforce their happy behavior. Go for a walk or play a favorite game. Read a book together. It doesn't have to be much, just something to let them know that when they are happy, their company is welcome—and that they will be given attention when they have good attitudes. When you do not put energy into their negative behavior and you reinforce their positive behavior, you'll find that your children express positively more and more of the time.

Be careful that you don't program fatness into your children by always rewarding them with food or using food to bribe them into good behavior. If you do that in any consistent way, the child is going to end up with a weight problem. Find a few alternatives. Find what the child likes to do and use that as a reward. Maybe the child likes to go swimming or miniature golfing or play at the park or get a new book or listen to some favorite music. These things are fun and can be used as a "reward" much more effectively than food.

One very important element in the whole concept of disciplining children is *love*. When you discipline children, you must always discipline out of your *love,* not out of your lack, and not out of your anger or your frustration. One reason that you should discipline children is to hold them to their levels of responsibility and teach them how to get along more effectively with themselves and others. You discipline out of your love and concern for the children.

If you spank your children in frustration because you cannot control them, the children will feel your frustration and anger coming at them and say, "You don't love us." Then they learn fear because they don't know whether or not they can trust you—and they can't feel your love. If you have laid out their guidelines, however, and they have not followed them, then it is your responsibility to bring them into line. If you do it in love, they'll know that—and they will not be hurt. Mock up your "anger" so you can be effective in your discipline. Be sure that it is a role that you're playing; you do this by keeping the loving going inside as you play out anger on the outside.

Discipline your children before the anger gets inside, before it controls you. When you find yourself yelling at your child, check very carefully and see if you're yelling at the child or at your own emotions that are pushing on you. Check to see if you would have had the same reaction if the child had done the same thing yesterday or last week. Maybe it didn't bother you yesterday, but today it does. So you're not really yelling at the child; you're yelling at your own irritation. This may confuse the child. The best thing to do is to explain to the youngster, "It's not really you I'm yelling at. I'm just upset today, and what you did irritated me more than I would have liked."

So many parents are afraid of appearing human or imperfect in front of their children. Then the children grow up thinking Mom and Dad are perfect and that they have to be perfect, too, to make Mom and Dad proud. That's a heavy burden to put on kids. If children know that Mom and Dad go through rough times, too, they'll know that is normal. Then they'll feel more freedom just to be what they are—and that's perfect. They'll know that they're still worthy of your love, even if they make a mistake. They'll be able to stay away from creating false images as protection. They'll be able to just be themselves and give and take love as the right and proper way to live life. It's important that you teach your children that mistakes are okay as part of this physical level and that they are correctable. Don't be afraid to apologize to your children. You can make mistakes, too. They'll still love you.

When you yell at your children, you are probably not being too effective in changing their behavior. Often, particularly with young children, they are really not sure of what you are yelling about. They may not understand the words. So you must do something besides yell, if you are to be effective. If you just yell and don't follow through physically, children won't pay any attention to you at all. They'll just think, "That person yells," and they'll go on doing what they want to do. Yelling upsets you more than it does the children, because they don't have any reference points.

If your child is up on some furniture where he is not supposed to be, you can say, "Billy, get down." At the same time, you walk over to him, pick him up, and put him down on the floor. As you do that, you say, "This means get down. When you hear me say, 'get down,' this is what I mean. Do you understand?" Then you can put him back up on the furniture and say, "Get down." If he doesn't move, you move him and again say, "This means get down." Then you might climb on something and tell him to tell you to get down. When he says, "Get down," you get down. Then put him up again and say, "Get down." You make it like a game, and pretty soon you have his cooperation. He learns it. And the next time you say, "Get down," he'll move.

Children who are spanked when it is necessary are never really hurt. They know when they're out of line, and they must be taught responsibility for their actions. They must be taught that they are creators and that they create what comes to them. So if they have been told that they are not supposed to tease their baby sister and they know that, they will get everything that goes along with the teasing if they continue to do that. It may be a spanking. It may be that some privilege is taken away from them. Whatever it is, you must be consistent in administering the discipline. If you are not consistent, the children will never know where the boundaries are and will continually test you to find out what today's boundary lines are. Then you will really have your hands full. If the boundaries are always the same, the children will be able to function very contentedly within them.

When you have disciplined your children for something and you feel badly about it later, you have probably over-disciplined them or disciplined them out of your anger rather than out of your love. If you feel good about it later, like "that was necessary," then you were probably right on the button with the discipline. You can usually tell by your inner responses if you're doing okay. If you discipline out of your own anger and frustration, then it's a poor form of discipline because you're disciplining the wrong person—you should be disciplining *yourself*. If the discipline is a teaching mechanism for the children, then listen very closely to the feelings within you as you discipline them.

Be careful that you don't start out with a form of pretended anger and then find yourself caught up in it and over-doing the discipline. When you discipline children, explain to them what is taking place and why, even if they don't understand on the same level that you are explaining. They'll understand on some level. Say. "I'm going to have to discipline you because you can't get into that medicine; it might harm you. The discipline is going to be easier than the harm would be. You must be made aware that it can harm you, and I love you too much to let you harm yourself. That's why this discipline is coming to you."

Sometimes you might spank children. Sometimes it will just be very firmly picking them up and holding them firmly. That can convey much more than a hit because you are forcing them into a listening position. If you hit them, they duck; they're not listening because they're protecting themselves. Then you hit them again because the first one didn't do it. Instead, take their face in your hands and turn them to look at you; do this gently and firmly, and say, "Listen to me. You cannot do that any longer. That will hurt you and I love you too much to let you be hurt." Let them know the discipline. They might not understand all the words; they will understand the love, however.

After you set certain boundaries for your children's behavior, you must keep the boundaries for the children until they can keep them for themselves. If you don't keep the boundaries constant, they will find no value in them. You must be consistent and persistent. Don't set up a discipline that you're not going to enforce or you will destroy all their confidence in you. Then you'll lose them by the time they're teenagers, if not sooner. You'll reap the whirlwind, and there will be nothing you can do. The crucial time is when they're young.

When a child reaches a certain age of its own willfulness (or "won't-fulness"), it may become more difficult to set guidelines and have them followed. The child may say, "I won't pay any attention to your guidelines. I won't do what you say, and you can't make me." If this is carried out to an extreme, the child must be turned over to an organized group that has the sanction of the society to intervene and bring forward the training and the discipline that is necessary to bring the child into the next level of his or her development.

Many parents feel a great sense of betrayal and failure if their children must come under the authority of the juvenile courts or the police. There is no reason to feel that type of concern or judgment, however.

Sometimes children come in with karma that is more severe than their parent's karma. There are certain patterns of expression and behavior that they must fulfill that were never part of their parent's experience. It can lead to hurt and confusion in both the children and the parents if not looked at clearly. The parents wonder, "Why are my children so bad? I wasn't like that.

My parents weren't like that. What have we done wrong?" The children are different than you. They have their own levels of responsibility to their own incarnation lines, and they must fulfill these.

Don't wish that your children be just like you. Have the wit to wish that they fulfill their destiny in the best possible way for them. And wish that you have the wit to assist them, not block them. This doesn't mean that you let your kids run wild and then hand them over to the juvenile courts—not at all! You do all that you can do to bring them into a balance of expression and discipline and to teach them the normal guidelines of society. If all you can do is not enough and your children seem to need that extra measure of authority, don't berate yourself and judge yourself as a failure. It may be that the experience is necessary for them.

Keep in mind that when you discipline children, you're working for their highest good. A lot of people don't realize that. They're only after a "now" response, and that's not always for the highest good. It should be as though you were in a big balloon, looking at a vision of your children's lives over a long span. You look at those things that will be good in the long run. It's easy to give in and let them eat the candy today; the question is, how is their health going to be in five or ten years? In what condition are their teeth going to be? You're responsible for looking ahead and doing the things that have to be done today—now—to fulfill the vision. The children are not old enough or wise enough to do that for themselves. That's your job—to teach them and explain to them in detail why you're doing things and what the proposed benefits will be for them. Then they won't feel you're being capricious and arbitrary when you're placing out the rules for them.

The early years of growing up are most important. If you haven't loved and disciplined your children by the time they're ten, you can just about forget it. You've probably already lost them. When they're little, they must know that you're there, that you love them, that you care, that they can trust you, and that you're the one they can count on. When your children ask you questions, give them honest answers. Don't put them off with excuses or lies or anything else. Take the time to educate them and explain this world to them.

Society is so full of educational information that if you think you can tell your kids the facts of life when they're fourteen, you'll be way too late. By fourteen they can probably *demonstrate* the facts of life. Some people still think what was good enough for their parents and for themselves will be good enough for their children—"They can learn about the facts of life when they get married." By that time, it's far too late. Children do not have to learn about sexual things through experience, however. You can teach them a lot through open, honest discussion. Let them ask questions, tell you what's on their minds, and communicate.

Eventually, your children are going to experience sex for themselves to find out the things that can't be told to them. If you are honest in giving your children sex education, you may be able to allow them to bypass the sexual experience until they're ready to handle it emotionally. Many youngsters who get into early sexual encounters are not ready to handle those experiences emotionally or mentally, and sometimes it turns out that they are not ready to handle it financially or physically, either. There are responsibilities and potential responsibilities on many levels that go with sexual intimacy, and children should be intelligently educated to be aware of these things.

The spiritual energy and the creative-sexual urge reside side-by-side in the reproductive area of the body between the thigh and the navel in a band around the body. So when the consciousness of Spirit activates itself, it may stir the sexual area of the body. It may cause irritation and excitation in that area, and this can cause the child to feel, to check, to see what is going on. Then the basic self is aroused and seeks to find a release for those energies. The basic self equates the feeling with sex. Youngsters should be told these things; they have a right to know what is taking place within them. Explain it to them. Explain what is going on within their consciousnesses and their bodies. When they don't want to hear anymore, you'll see them drop that thing over their eyes that says, "Forget it; don't talk anymore; I'm not listening." You all know what that look is. You experienced it. You all did it to your folks. They did it to theirs. We all have this inheritance. When you see your child's attention drop away, let it go. Come back to it later, if they ask you. For God's sake and for the sake of that child, tell them the truth. Use terms that they know. And don't put shock value on any word that relates to the human body. If they call it a certain word, use that word; it's a word they know and understand. If you use words that are special or educational, they'll think you're afraid to talk about it.

There is an interesting fact about so-called "dirty words." Let's say your youngster of six years old comes home from school and uses the word "shit" in front of you. You get upset and reprimand him for saying that "naughty word" or that "nasty word." So they identify that word with something bad.

Then later, when you're angry with him, you say, "You're nothing but a little shit." The very action of calling him that name tells him that he's bad and nasty and no-good. It's a heavy thing. Then when you tell him you love him, he's confused. He doesn't know what you mean.

It's important that you do not put out value judgments on names or words, or go into shock if your child uses any particular word. They're just words. If they bother you, go and stand in front of a mirror and say them over and over and over until they lose their power over you. Then you'll be able to direct your child into better speech expressions, rather than just reacting when he says something "dirty."

If your children seem to be trying to get attention and are determined to have their own way, you can sometimes select an area which won't do any harm and let them have their way, totally, in that area. If they want a lot of ice cream, let them have it—all they want. They'll just throw it up. If they get stomach aches, let them know those experiences go along with eating a lot of ice cream. You don't have to worry. They won't die of stomach aches. Check to see if your children's requests are reasonable. If they are, and they do not conflict with your plans, there's no reason to not let them have what they request.

One time I was visiting a sea-life entertainment center and saw a man and his wife and their little girl standing by one of the exhibits. The little girl was too little to see into the fish tank where they were, and the parents kept making comments about what they were seeing there. She was fussing and crying, "I want to see, I want to see," and the parents were shushing her up. I walked over and picked her up and held her so she could see into the tank. The father looked at me in surprise and said, "What are you doing?"

I said, "I'm holding her up so she can see. She wanted to see and her request is not unreasonable."

He said, "You're absolutely right," and he took the child and held her where she could see. They hadn't been paying any attention to her. They were more concerned with their own comfort and entertainment than they were with the child. It's an area that you have to watch carefully.

If your baby wants to pull all the pots and pans out of the cupboard, that's not unreasonable. It's not going to hurt anything. The baby will learn what they are. The youngster also gets to help put them all back—and that's important. Help the child explore the house. Spend some time with the child. Let them take all the towels out of the linen closet, and then show them how to fold and put them back. If the child doesn't do it perfectly, who cares? You can put the towels back correctly the next time you use them. Children are just trying to learn about this world as fast as they can. If you help them in their learning, you'll be much further ahead, and so will they.

Don't ever tell your children, "Clean up your room so God will love you," or "Clean up your room so Daddy will be proud of you." Tell them, "Clean up your room because I want you to." That's honest, and it's reasonable. They'll clean up their rooms because you want them to. It makes more sense to clean it up for you than it does to clean it up for God. Don't tell the kids,

"Eat everything on your plate because people around the world are starving." They don't understand about those people who are starving; they can't relate to that. Tell them, "Eat the food because I want you to, because I love you and want you to be healthy." If they don't want to eat it, don't force them. We have a lot of overweight people in this country who were so programmed by their parents to eat all their food that they can't stop it now, even when they want to.

If you have educated your kids well, you can ask them to turn off the television because it's giving you a headache; even though they may not want to, they will do what you ask. They will know it's a reasonable request because it's making you feel bad. They will know that the world won't always let them listen to their own level as loudly as they might like to, and they're going to have to cooperate. Then discipline comes in as reality, and they say, "You have been educating me all along."

Some people say, "I'm going to protect my children. I won't send them to that school." That attitude may be overprotective. Children are going to have to deal with all sorts of people and situations when they're older. They might as well learn how when they're young. You can protect them by loving them and always letting them know they can count on you to support them and assist them. You can't protect them by denying their experiences of learning and growth; you will suffer the consequences later, and so will your children.

A dear friend of mine came to me and said, "I don't know about putting my daughter in that school."

I said, "Put her in that school."

She said, "But some of the kids in that school are rough."

I said, "There are people who are rough in stores, on the streets; it happens all over."

She said, "But what if she gets her feelings hurt, or learns things that I don't want her to know about? What do I do if she comes home saying swear words? What if she gets bullied and hurt? I don't want her around tough kids; I want the best for my daughter."

I said, "When you were coming to see me today, you almost got in a car accident. Your daughter could have been hurt then."

She said, "Oh, my God." She really didn't have to say any more than that.

I said, "Do you constantly tell your daughter to be careful, and not play rough, and not be around kids you don't approve of so she doesn't get hurt?"

She said, "Yes."

I said, "You are promoting her getting hurt and getting involved in the very things you want her to avoid. She will be attracted into those things because that is what she is thinking about and that is her fear. I have said many times, what you fear comes upon you. You are focusing her attention on what you *don't* want for her to be involved in. Instead, why not tell her that God loves her, she is under spiritual protection, and nothing will hurt her? Show her how to put the Light around herself for protection. Teach her to send Light and loving to people and situations around her. It's OK to teach her to be watchful. Do it in a way that keeps her attention on what she wants. She will automaticaly stay away from what she doesn't want because her attention is directing her elsewhere. Let her know that experiences come to help her understand and grow and lift. Explain that experiences give her confidence in herself; she is learning to keep her wits about her and use everything for her advancement. You are giving her a powerful gift with that attitude, and supporting her in developing a sense of security that comes from the inside; it can't be taken away by the whims of the world. Explain these things to her, and she will be fine." That is the reality that a child can live, learn and grow with.

Chapter 4

Family

&

Home

Home should be a place that you can go to plug into a "battery" and recharge your life so that you can come out again into the world and do the best work you can. When you get tired, you should be able to go home, lie down, and regather your energies to go back out into the world. This is one reason it's important that the home be a stable, supportive environment. Sometimes a spouse will come home from work and open the door, only to be hit in the head by the other spouse, sometimes literally, sometimes verbally or emotionally. Sometimes the spouse present uses the spouse absent as blackmail against the children, saying, "Just wait till your mother (or father) gets home. You'll really be in trouble." So the kid becomes fearful about who is going to come through the door and knows that even at home, he's going to get it.

Years ago I was working with a young boy about sixteen years old, and we used to call him "hell on wheels" because of the way he handled his bike and his car. No one got in *his* way. He was always in trouble because of one thing or another. It was explained to him that he was approaching life in a way that was almost bound to bring himself injury and harm. He was told, "If you don't change, you are going to hurt yourself."

I had become friends with the boy's parents during the time I was working with him, and one night they invited me to dinner. I got there about half an hour before the young man did, and when he came in, both his parents pounced on him. "Why are you so late?

You are always doing this. Have you got your studies done? You didn't make your bed this morning." Yakadeeyakadeeyakadeeyak. I walked up to the young man and said, "If I were you, I'd move. I wouldn't put up with this."

The parents said, "What are you saying? You're disrupting our family!"

I said, "I couldn't possibly disrupt this family. You've done that already."

The boy was very upset and embarrassed that he was getting yelled at in front of me; he was also very amazed that I would be trying to assist him rather than change him. The parents said, "Well, let's all sit down to eat."

I said, "Good. That's what I came for; I didn't come to listen to you verbally beat your boy. Before we eat, let me just tell you what I see here. Why should this boy come home when he can't get the love and support he needs here, when he can't get himself recharged here? Why shouldn't he go someplace else? He's not getting what he needs here at home, so he goes someplace else and gets charged the wrong way. Then he is out running around the city trying to disperse the energy. He's doing the best he can with what he's got. It's hard out there in the world. It's hard for him. He has people picking on him all the time because of his behavior. He doesn't know what to do about it. So he comes home for comfort and support, and you pick on him. Where can he go? Where is he going to go to get the kind of energy he needs to compete in this world?"

The boy's mother and father broke down in tears. The boy sat there and looked at me and started fidgeting in his seat, thinking, "Oh, God, my parents are crying." I looked at him and said, "Remember that it is only people who are really men and women who have the ability to cry. It's only little sneaks like you who are ashamed to see honesty being demonstrated." And then *he* broke down in tears.

His parents looked up and said, "What can we do?"

The boy said, "Don't yell at me when I come in the door."

They said, "Okay, and can you make your bed?"

He said, "Sure, I can make my bed. I don't because it's the one way I can get back at you. I can't yell back; you'd hit me."

They said, "Will you listen to us when we talk to you?"

He said, "I'll listen if you don't yell at me. I want to hear what you have to say; you've fed me, given me clothes, and given me money to do things."

They said, "You appreciate that?"

He said, "Sure. It's just that you never give me a chance to say so. I am always defending myself, trying to show that I have some kind of dignity inside of me."

They said, "Is there anything else?"

He said, "No."

When I saw that making the bed was a problem, I said, "That's it? You yelled at this kid because of that?"

They said, "No, we also yelled because of his attitude."

I asked him, "What is your attitude?"

He said, "When I make the bed I moan and groan."

I said, "Okay, can you quit that?"

He said, "Sure, if they don't nag."

I said, "No, that's not good enough. They *should* nag if you don't make your bed. You slept there all night long, and the Lord slept there with you; that is a very special place. So you make the bed in the morning—lovingly and perfectly."

The boy said, "How do I do it?"

His Dad said, "I was in the military. I know how to make the bed." So in the midst of dinner we all stood up, went in the bedroom, pulled all the linens off, and his father showed him how to make the bed. Then his mother said, "Neither one of you know how to make a bed." She went over, ripped it up, and made it again. Then we all laughed. I was convinced it was the first honest-to-God laugh that had been heard in that house in a long time.

About this time I became aware that their daughter wasn't home yet. According to her mother and father, she was out a little bit too late for her age. They were talking about it. "Where is she? It's getting late. She should be home by now." They were starting to work themselves into a "panic," when I heard a car pull up in front of the house. I knew she was too young to drive, so I figured she was with somebody else. I wasn't too sure if her parents were paying attention, however, because they were too busy fighting her in their heads.

I went outside and met her on the front walk and said, "If I were you, I'd walk in there backwards."

She said, "Why?"

I said, "They're really disturbed with you, love."

She said, "My girlfriends and I just had a soda and met some boys. We were just talking and laughing and joking and practicing some cheerleading songs." She was so innocent. It was beautiful. I would want my daughter to do the same. It was a totally wholesome activity of being involved with her peers, learning what was going on, being accepted, and gaining a good attitude.

I said, "Let me go in first." So I opened the door and went in. Her mother and father were standing there and I thought, "Oh, oh, they think I'm their daughter." So I put up my hands and said, "Deflect." Then the humor started. The girl was right behind me, and she put her arms out under my arms and was reaching around and waving—like for a truce—and it was really funny. Her folks started laughing and they said, "Where have you been?" Then she started crying. She said, "That's the first time you've ever asked me where I've been. You've always *told* me where I'd been—like up to no good."

She was so relieved to have them ask her that she told them who she'd been with and where and really shared her experiences with them. Her parents said, "Did you have a good time?"

She said, "Yes, it was really neat."

They said, "That's nice. We're glad you're home safe." As I stood there watching all of this going on, I realized that I'd better leave. I wasn't part of the family and they didn't need me there anymore. They were busy rediscovering each other and their love.

It was too bad it all hadn't happened about five years sooner, because they had already promoted some things they would rather not have happen to their kids. The daughter had already promoted a pregnancy. She came to me a few weeks later and said, "What am I going to do?"

I said, "Go talk to your mother and father."

She said, "They'll kill me."

I said, "That'll solve your problem." I asked her if she wanted the baby. She said, "Yes, I want the baby. Maybe it'll be the only thing in this world I'll be able to love." And inwardly I thought of how her feelings regarding her parents had let her down and given her the feeling of betrayal so that she could only think of the baby in terms of someone for *her* to love—not in terms of who the baby would be and what it was to do in the world.

I asked her, "Will the baby love you?"

She said, "I hadn't even thought about that." I said,

"What about your love for your parents? Do you love them automatically just like your baby is supposed to love you automatically?"

She said, "Maybe I shouldn't have the baby—I don't know."

I said, "It's not a question of whether you should or shouldn't have the baby; it's a question of whether you can trust your parents enough to tell them about the baby."

She said, "It will destroy them. Good girls don't do this."

I said, "Oh, really? Since when?"

She said, "The boy doesn't want to marry me."

I said, "How do you know? Have you talked to him about this?" She hadn't. I said, "I happen to know a lady who 'trapped' her husband that way, and he was so glad she did that he didn't know what to do about it. So they had a whole bunch of kids just to prove their love."

She said, "That's old-folk stuff."

I said, "There is no such thing. It's only your attitude that's old-folky. This is real. You are going to have a child, and you better think some things through. Where do you plan to have the baby? Some relief society? Some health clinic? Some poverty clinic? Where? How are you going to support the child? Quit school? Go to work? How are you going to pay for a baby-sitter?"

She said, "I guess I'd better go talk to my mother and father."

I said, "That's about the best thing I've heard so far."

She said, "Will you come over?"

I said, "Sure. Get me a dinner invitation, and I'll come over."

Her mother was a good cook. I went to dinner and everybody was there. We sat down, and in the middle of dinner the daughter said, "I'm pregnant."
I thought, "There are so many ways to say it, and that is not one of them."
Her mother said, "What?"

Her father said, "What?"

She said, "I'm pregnant. You're going to be a grandma and grandpa."

They said, "Really?" Already the focus was changing from the idea of their daughter being pregnant to the idea that they were going to be grandparents; the baby was already welcome.

Her dad asked, "Who's the father?"

She said, "I'm not going to tell you."

He said, "Why not?"

She said, "Because good girls don't do what I've done."

He said, "Well, if you've got a good man, maybe good girls do that. Tell me who he is, honey."

She told him and he said, "He's a good man." They got married the next week and had a beautiful little child. If there is a moral to the story, it would be that you don't attempt to change people; you assist them where they are. They will change themselves out of their own love and thankfulness. It has always been that way. You may be able to force people to pretend they've changed, to look like they've knuckled down. That, however, is not a change that lifts life into a newer element of happiness.

You really do not have a right to judge other people. In fact, when you see anyone less fortunate than you, you can rightfully think, "There but for the grace of God, go I." Then you can attempt to understand and assist and help that other person. When you maintain your uprightness wherever you walk, people say, "Thank God you've been here. Please come back anytime."

A good indicator of success is whether people want you to become part of their lives on some basis. Let them set the rules and the definitions, and if you feel like you can participate without compromising your integrity, then you're clear. If it comes to the point where you don't feel clear, however, then do not participate on that level. Maintain your own individuality, your own integrity. Even if it turns out to be a wrong action, it's much easier to correct a mistake of omission than one of commission. It's much easier to say, "I'm really sorry I didn't make it," than to wish you'd never gone.

If you give people a chance to share things with you, you'll often have a lot of companionship. If you start telling them what to do and how to do it, however, you may find yourself alone again. People often do not like to be told what to do. If you can give them some direction and suggest things to them, however, and then extend your love and support to assist them—they'll be so lifted. And if they can't do it, assist them so they look good. They'll love to participate in your life. You know what that's called? Marriage! Marriage is that unconditional love that says, "I love you. It doesn't matter what you do. I'll just help you to be the best *you* you can be." It often seems that not too long after you get married, this action stops and becomes, *"Don't do it that way, you idiot!"*

So you say, "If I'm an idiot and you married me, what does that make you?" An idiot-lover, obviously.

The other says, "Well, you're not really an idiot. That was just my way of describing my dissatisfaction with your approach."

You say, "You weren't dissatisfied before we were married. My approach hasn't changed. So why don't you go do the things you have to do and let me do what I have to do. Then we can meet later and discuss it without calling each other names."

Communication is a big key in all relationships. If you have a headache and you're really not feeling well, tell your loved one that. If you're feeling grumpy and think that things are a little rocky in your consciousness, ask your spouse not to evaluate your life based upon this day. After all, you may feel different tomorrow. One or two days of feeling bad is not the verdict of a lifetime. You are always, constantly, in a state of rejuvenation. You are always evolving into a more positive, more loving you. That's your primary responsibility on this planet—to take care of yourself and to rise to your highest potential.

A mother and father can be two of your greatest teachers. They can teach you many things, on many levels. They teach you in whatever way is necessary for you to learn, and that is really a demonstration of great love. I remember years ago, during the depression, when my friend was working in the mines—and lucky to have a job of any kind. At that time, there were four little kids in his family. I was at his home one day, and I noticed his wife was having a hard day with the four kids. She was tired and fed up, and they really had her climbing the walls. (Have you ever seen a mother climb a wall? It's a delightful experience! Have you got the image? Wallpaper coming down....?)

The husband came home from work, and she sort of jumped at him as soon as he walked in the front door. She said, "I don't think I can take another day of this."

He said, "You don't have to. You can go anytime."

She said, "You don't love me." He handed her the paycheck. She said, "What's this?"

He said, "Tokenism."

She opened it up and said, "It's just the damned paycheck."

He said, "I worked damned hard for that damned paycheck, only to come home and have you complain."

At that point, she realized very deeply someplace inside of her that he really didn't have to come home and give her the paycheck. He didn't have to come home at all. He did, however. Then he asked her, "Would you like to go work in the mines and shovel coal, push the coal carts, dump it, load it onto the trucks, then run back up the hill, blast the coal, shovel it, push it out, dump it, load it, etcetera, for fifteen or sixteen hours a day?"

She said, "I prefer the kids." From that point on, it was her choice.

She never really complained very much after that. Their home became more thankful and more loving. The husband had to demonstrate to her the love that was in his heart all those hours that he was at work. I'm sure she thought he was up at the mine drinking with the guys and having a good time. He had enough love inside him to explain to her the way it was, from his inner reality.

Over the years, I saw their love stay in the home, and it was given to each child. When a child came home after trouble or a fight, he would be taken aside and given special time. The mother would take care of the cuts and bruises and make sure nothing was seriously wrong. The parents taught the kids well. They were told, in no uncertain terms, that they were to win the fight or not get into it. They learned at a very early age that being a peacemaker is joyful. To have peace in the heart is even more joyful. And then to share that peace is even more joyful. You can share the emotional understanding when you say, "I understand that, I've felt the same way." That's glorious, too.

Allowing God's Light to flow through your consciousness to others and awaken the Light that is within them is a transcendental experience. There are no words. Yet it is the most real state of being that there is, and in that state you can do no wrong. You can do only right. Many marriages are based on emotional immaturity, a level of lack within one or both partners that they are looking to the other person to fill and satisfy. It doesn't work that way. Marriages that are based upon emotional immaturity rarely last, unless both partners manage to "grow up" together. That seldom happens. For a marriage to be successful, both people must recognize that their fulfillment comes from within themselves. The other person may enhance their completeness; they don't supply it, however. When each marriage partner gives one hundred percent into the marriage, it is a beautiful, working marriage.

A wife I know used to exercise what I call the "tyranny of weakness." She would say, "I have a headache. I can't do that." Through this weakness, she'd become the tyrant. One time she was doing this and I started to laugh. She said, "Why are you laughing?"

I said, "It amazes me that you are so beautiful and so smart and one of the most skilled seamstresses and designers in this area, yet you don't have the intelligence to get rid of your headache. It makes me laugh." She got up and took a couple of aspirin to get rid of the headache. I said, "What excuse are you going to use now?"

One day the husband came home when she had a terrible headache. He walked in the door and said, "Oh, God, I've got a terrible headache."

She said, "You can't! I had it first."

He looked at her and the Light lit up in his eyes. He laughed and said, "Ah-ha, I see what is going on." Then he went in the kitchen and fixed her a cup of coffee, scrambled some eggs and made toast, and put a beautiful flower on the table.

She said, "Oh, honey, that flower should be in a vase with some water." He said, "You can keep your headache!"

She said, "No, wait a minute." She got a vase with some water and put the flower in it. That wasn't worth a fight. She sat there and ate the food.

Later, the husband asked, "How do you feel now?"

She said, "I think we should talk about my headache a little more. I think my headache needs to be respected and appreciated. I think it needs a drive in the country and dinner out tonight. I think my headache needs love with my husband." It was amazing how her headache improved with tender loving care. If people close to you are not feeling well, do whatever you can to make them feel better. It's worth it. It can be a lot of fun if your attitude is right. They will look at you, and when that Light of God comes through them, you'll have your reward—if you need any reward beyond the opportunity to share your love.

There is a spiritual law that says you get what you give. So if you want to receive love, give love. If you want to see love, you must have love inside of you as you look into the world. See love everywhere you look. To see love, you have to let go of greed and envy and jealousy. Nobody said it was easy. If it were, you would already have done it. It's a challenge that is worth undertaking, however. When you undertake this challenge of living love, the by-product is success.

When you honestly attempt to maintain your life, to live your life, to enhance your life, and to make your life work for you in the best way possible, then the thing we call *living love* just stands up inside of you and sings joyously. People turn around and say, "What have you been doing? You look so good." Then you can share with them those things that are working for you.

Everyone wants freedom, liberation, and the ability to be comfortable in the body and in the emotions. If you feel like you can't say, "I love you" to someone you do love, then go stand in front of a mirror and say, "I love you, I love you, I love you, I love you"—until you break through that block. Go stand on a rooftop and yell, "I love you." If you feel silly, then stand in front of the mirror and say, "I'm silly, I'm silly, I'm silly,"—until you just don't care anymore. Don't let your emotions block you from honest, loving expression. Love is part of your emotional structure, and you can use your love to help heal the world. You can certainly use it to bring healing to yourself and those close to you. *With enough love, nothing is impossible.*

When you are in the consciousness of living love, you get to demonstrate that love to everyone and everything that comes your way. Maybe you pat some people on the back and tell them you appreciate the good job they've done. That may stay with them for a long, long time. That may lift them more than you'll ever know. That love that you demonstrate becomes a constant reference point for you and them.

When you start to find the truth of your expression and your environment, you get to take out those things that aren't working, put in the things that are working, and have the wit to know which is which. You gain wisdom by practice, practice, practice. There is no other way. Yes, it's trial and error for quite awhile. You finally learn what it is, and then you demonstrate your wisdom by changing your behavior. Then people say, "What a wise person!" They just can't see the black-and-blue marks you have from not being so wise. That's part of being human. The bruises are badges of courage, of doing, of involvement, of communication.

Don't retreat from life in the fear that you'll be hurt. If you get hurt, you'll recover. If you retreat, however, you may fall back into something of which you were supposed to beware. Keep moving forward. Keep your awareness open and watch. Take care of yourself and those close to you.Don't hurt anyone, and don't allow anyone to hurt you. Support and assist everyone you come in contact with. That's living love.

Some people are not equipped to handle a deep, emotional, sustained, loving commitment. So that one who is a skilled lover, who walks arm and arm with the Beloved, knows how to move in and out, come close and then move away. In this way a skilled lover brings new life and joy to his or her loved one, instead of a sustained pressure that produces tension and resistance.

Pressure can cause you to cry out, "For God's sake, leave me alone!" Then as the other person backs off, you say, "No, wait, I didn't mean that." You don't want the person to leave you alone; you just want them to allow you a little space. You're really saying, "Just be tender, love me, let me breathe, and let me feel that wonderful, free flowing loving inside of me."

Children who cry are not only crying for food and a change of diapers; they are crying for love to be demonstrated to them. The nature of children is love. Love is natural to them—as it is to all of us. Some people really are bashful about feeling or expressing their love. They're ashamed of those deep, true feelings inside of them. That's nothing to be ashamed of. That's God. When you just love, with no restrictions, no qualifications, no conditions—just love for each moment and with every breath—you'll be so happy and so joyful, you'll have a hard time containing it all. When this type of love is in the home, that's the place you come to charge yourself so you can go back out in the world and do those things that must be done.

Many years ago I had the chance to take a young man home from school. He had been in a fight. He was really upset and was hurting. I took him home and explained to his parents what had happened. They were already starting to jump on him and berate him for what had happened. I said, "Wait a minute. If you want to beat him up, wait until I leave. You're not going to beat him up—physically or verbally—while I'm here, however. I would like you to think about a couple of things before you say anything more to him: Do you want him to come home from school tomorrow? Do you want him to be afraid to come home, or do you want him to look forward to coming home? He's been beat up rather severely today. He doesn't need another beating. He needs a warm bath and food and somebody to take care of him. He doesn't need anyone to cuss him or berate him. What are you trying to do to this young man? Cripple him emotionally? Push him away? Where is he going to get love if you don't give it to him? Do you want him to go out to the streets looking for the love he can't find here?"

His parents said, "I guess you're right. He has to have support from home. If we don't give it to him here, who will?"

I said, "I will; it won't be the same as if you do it, however."

When your children come home from school, make sure that home is the playground, the paradise. Home does represent the kingdom of heaven to children. It's the place to refuel and charge up their batteries. As the family is strong in its nature, the community gets strong. As the community gets strong, society gets strong. As society gets strong, culture and civilization grow, and spirituality moves in. It is on *love* that all these things are built.

If you are married, be the "superwife" or "superhusband" when your spouse comes home. Sometimes that's just as simple as rubbing his or her back. You say, "Rub their back? I need mine rubbed!" Okay, after you rub theirs, they rub yours. If you say, "Why should I rub theirs first?" that's the barter system, and you lose. That's not love.

Do you really love the guy or gal you're married to? If you do, it won't matter who rubs whose back first. If it's really love, the question will never even come up. These loving things will just take place.

Families are brought together to refine and sandpaper each other. Chipping and hitting aren't necessary. To refine the consciousness and then to move that refined consciousness into the soul and allow the consciousness to have awareness of soul, however—that is magnificent. That's the goal of the family. Then you will know that you are an essence of God, an extension of God.

When you fight with your spouse or your children, you fight the God within them and within you. You cause separation. Sometimes you want to fight to awaken your loved one and say, "I see so much in you; I want to shake you loose so you'll see what I see." Why don't you love them loose instead? Why don't you make your love so dynamic that without it they could not survive? With that love, you all go together into the heart of God.

Bibliography

Items are audio tapes unless otherwise noted. V preceding a number denotes the tape is also available in video format. SAT stands for Soul Awareness Tapes, which are audio tapes of J-R seminars, meditations, and sharings that are sent each month only to SAT subscribers. Once you subscribe, you can obtain previously issued tapes.

- Can a Child Lead Them? (#7256, SAT Tape)
- Can a Marriage Be Threatened? (#2626)
- Communication in a Safe Space (#7536)
- The Divine Communion (#3212)
- Guidelines in Dealing with People (#2615)
- How Did Materialism Start in You? (#7024)
- How Guilt is Built and its Effects (#1704)
- J-R Talks to Teens (#3407)
- Relationships: Rescuing You or Saving Me? (#7044, SAT tape)
- Relationships: The Art of Making Life Work (Book, #951-5)
- Sexual-Spiritual Responsibilities & Hoo Chant (#2055)
- Social-Sexual Behavior (#7186, SAT Tape)
- The Spiritual Marriage (#2105)
- The Three Selves (#1208)

OTHER - Ongoing Spiritual Study

● MSIA on the Internet at http://www.msia.com

The web site offers a free subscription to MSIA's daily inspirational e-mail, Loving Each Day; the *New Day Herald* online; the opportunity to request that names be placed on the prayer list; MSIA's catalog, and much more.

● Soul Awareness Discourses

If you like this book, Discourses are a gold mine of further information. Here is a sample of the contents: communication in Discourse 99; discipline in Discourses 44 and 77; highest good in Discourses 2 and 109; speaking kind words in Discourse 50; three selves in Discourse 17; and much more. (Twelve books per year, one for each month, English, Spanish, or French, #5000).

● Soul Awareness Tape (SAT) Series

A new John-Roger seminar every month, plus access to the entire SAT library of hundreds of meditations & seminars. (Twelve tapes per year, one sent each month, #5400)

OTHER - Ongoing Spiritual Study *(cont.)*

- Forgiveness, The Key to the Kingdom (Book, #934-3)
- Manual on Using the Light (Book, 960-2)
- Soul Journey through Spiritual Exercises (Three tape album with booklet; #3718)
- Spiritual Exercises: Walking with the Lord (Four tape album, #3907)
- *Spiritual Warrior: The Art of Spiritual Success* (Book, available in book-stores everywhere, ISBN 0-914829-36-X)
- *The Path to Mastership* (Book, #957-2)
- *The Power Within You* (Book, #924-6)
- *The Tao of Spirit* (Book, #933-5)

Tapes and books are available from:
MSIA®
P.O. Box 513935
Los Angeles, CA 90051
213-737-4055   FAX 213-737-5680
soul@msia.org
http://www.msia.org

About the Author

Since 1963, John-Roger has traveled all over the world, lecturing, teaching, and assisting people who want to create a life of greater health, happiness, peace, and prosperity and a greater awakening to the Spirit within. His humor and practical wisdom have benefited thousands and lightened many a heart.

In the course of this work, he has given over 5,000 seminars, many of which are televised nationally on "That Which Is." He has also written more than 35 books, including co-authoring two *New York Times* best-sellers.

The common thread throughout all John-Roger's work is loving, opening to the highest good of all, and the awareness that God is abundantly present and available.

If you've enjoyed this book, you may want to explore and delve more deeply into what John-Roger has shared about this subject and other related topics. See the bibliography for a selection of study materials. For an even wider selection of study materials and more information on John-Roger's teachings through MSIA, please contact us at:

MSIA®
P.O. Box 513935
Los Angeles, CA 90051-1935
(213) 737-4055
soul@msia.org
http://www.msia.org